SUNRISES AT MIDNIGHT

SUNRISES AT MIDNIGHT

GIN LOVE THOMPSON

ON
YX
INK PRESS

ONYX INK PRESS
New York, New York 10019

Library of Congress Control Number: 2019906501

ISBN-13: 978-0-9855992-7-0

ISBN-10: 0-9855992-7-8

Copy editor: Doug Powers

Cover design: Jesse Hayes hayesdesignstudios.com

Dedicated to Prince Rogers Nelson for being a reflection of what I was not yet able to see in myself.

For you...

The radiance of enlightenments
are oft unearthed
amidst the darkest of nights…
sunrises at midnight.

CONTENTS

Foreword

Sunrises at Midnight is the first of what we anticipate being a continued anthology of poetic pieces authored by Gin Love Thompson. Immerse yourself in her dynamic expressions caught in moments in time. Her poetry is a portal into phases in Gin's emotional journey that evokes pulses of pain, flows of fear and memories that both crush and elevate beyond the stars. Gin gracefully exposes her soul. She taps into man's inhumanity; she bathes you in oceans. Jump in. Enjoy the ride!

Samaria Graham
June 3, 2019

Actress and Activist, NBC's Providence and Blossom, CBS miniseries Shake, Rattle and Roll: An American Love Story, featured performer on title-track of Tupac Shakur compilation, *The Rose That Grew From Concrete*

BELONGING

It is as vital to know where
you no longer belong
as it is to know where
you do belong.

PART I

FLUIDITY

Beloved

Beloved, have you been betrayed
Has your deep heart been invaded
Unaware by a thief in the night
Has your Soul been bruised
By the beating of a heavy heart
The gentle nature of your kiss
Ravaged by the bite of bitterness
Oh my Love, I ask only this:
Embrace yourself today
Open the portals of pain
So they may flow away
Breathe in the sacred touch
Of the ultimate Lover's call
Washing you from all stains
As the caress of its rains fall
Allow it to drench you
Take it within your pores
You are One to be adored
Suffer no more
Love is here, open the door.

DESTINY

Know the mountain
you're climbing, intimately.
It will still bring unexpected terrain,
though when it is your mountain
you will recognize it by touch.

It will call to you.
You will not have to search
endlessly for its location.

It will appear before you
in the Eye of your Soul.
You will know it is yours.

Beyond That Field

Holding fast to images,
countless dream filled days.
Sun rays shimmer,
as diamonds glimmer
upon the lilies of that field.

Meet me out beyond where
the Sufis led us to,
where right and wrong doing
continue to elude.

Where our thoughts wrapped
in jade colored papers
remain fresh, unspoiled.

Where exhilaration consumes
in the arms of continual mornings,
in moments of glory, joyful reprise,
as we look toward
tomorrow's crimson sunrise.

Searching out the beauty,
even that disguised within pain,
remembering the journey
of a thousand different names.

Meet me out beyond where
the Sufis led us to,
where Love and peace
were all that we knew.

RECONNECT

Often, we pause to gather ourselves. In those times we reconnect to pieces we have forgotten. Simultaneously, we release others that no longer fit. Make no mistake about it, my darling, deep inside behind the fear and confusion is you; is Love. Remember, you are bigger than this planet can hold, for you truly are made of the dust of stars. It is not a poetic placidity —you have proven it to yourself countless times. This too shall pass and you will be fully in Love with life again. Those moments make everything else worth it.

F IREFLY

There is so much darkness in the world;
be the Light.

Be the firefly of a summer's night
that reminds Souls of the miracle of life.

Wear the colors of the monarch's wings
in your smile.

Send hearts soaring.
Be Love.

G RATITUDE

Peace is but a breath away,
stillness of the quiet mind,
priceless treasure

Joyful in the eternal now
releasing desire,
parting with strife

Focusing on gratitude,
seeing, appreciating
the beauty in all of life

With Eye of Light
we need not physical sight.
Reaching toward calmness,
surrounded by Love,
accepting no less

As you travel this sacred journey,
be selective of your guests.

My Love

My Love is like a river
it bends,
continuously flows
connective with the ocean
oneness with the Soul.

My Love is like the song bird,
sonorous with joy
imploring you to hear
blissful to be near.

My Love is like the rain that falls,
infused with grace
tender drops of protection
saturate.

My Love is like the mountains,
energy pulsating
ensconcing you in their strength.

My Love is like the moon
reflecting the Light of you.

My Love is like the universe
for this is where it was born,
empirically adorned,
cosmically expansive
—infinite, eternal.

My Love.

Navy Night

Visiting deeply rooted trees
On a luminous navy night
Embraced within branches
Fertile from the soil of truth
Star children reaching toward Heaven
Beneath its starlight
Under the skies hushed cries
Visions of tantric orgasm
Transpose to electric blue
Stardust filling my eyes
In this cosmic bedroom
Waves of turquoise encircle
Dripping with evening's dew
Cradled in this supernatural groove.

R EMEMBERING

Above the clouds
Sailing to the moon
Did I ever tell you
I lassoed it just for you
There's nothing I wouldn't do
Love takes center stage
Spotlight on Samadhi
Embracing moon beams shimmer
Peace of yin and yang
Never has it faltered
Balance of constant change
Loving, letting go
They are often one in the same
Embracing natures flow
The impermanence of tomorrow
Cannot wilt the bloom of now
For Love is but an action
Of God's invisible hand
We can be the vessel
If we are courageous
Enough to understand

Above the clouds
Sailing past today
Remembering the fragrance
Of Love given away.

FROM MY WOMB

I taught you how to treat me,
now I am teaching you once again
back then I was all for you,
not yet my own friend

Pouring out of heart
captivated in Love for you
never entering my mind
one day you could seek to consume

Self Love my lesson
I thank you for helping me find
necessary communion
plunged into chasms of heart and mind

How many years of tears
awaiting a true return
frozen in awaiting you
while abiding awaited a multitude

No expectations, no longer asking why
some things aren't meant to be
releasing you to the sky
allowing us all to fly free

This freedom is bittersweet,
cleansing stinging rain
purifying painful years
removing every stain

Praying the truth I planted
within you will guide eternally
riding on wings of Love,
look higher, that's where I will be.

THE ESSENCE

I haven't time for nonverbal lies
Emotions dripping with regret
Shredded by deceit
Love's taken over
The why, the how
They're not important now
Only need today
Nothing's slipping away
All that's enduring remains.

THE LONGING

What do you do with it?
The loss.

Where do you neatly tuck it away in
your life
where the creases do not show
allowing appearance to remain
crisp, neat.

Where do you hide it so life can just
pick up, move on
—get back to it all.

How do you dry the tears
of tangible life energy no longer present,
of change that wreaks havoc.

The human condition of pretending
staunchly, our hidden grimacing
with collars up, heads held high
while inside we are all longing for
something.

Someone.

Morning Dawns

The world moves on
within the ravages
of the unforeseeable storm
You think it would stop,
skip a beat

Unlike a scarred album
it continues to spin
No pauses over scratches
no matter how profound
no distortion of sound
as your heart hits the ground

Fireworks still explode in the skies
as part of you dies.

Morning dawns life moves on
A new day to move and sway
It doesn't have to all go your way
To be a beautiful day

Looking up at the stars
knowing once our eyes view
they've already burned away

Poignant isn't it
Even after we are gone
our actions determine
life's continuing song,
what shines on
in the darkness of night

revealing passages
beneath eternal twilight

Morning dawns life moves on
A new day to move and sway
It doesn't have to all go your way
To be a beautiful day

We survive harsh realities
every day
Only needing enough Light
in the coolness of midnight
to steady our way

Warm hands that never harm
from the fire they bring
Ensconced in safe arms
absorbed in moments of Love
that never stings
In this the healing heart sings

These are a few
of my favorite things.

Morning dawns life moves on
A new day to move and sway
It doesn't have to all go your way
To be a beautiful day

I WILL REMEMBER YOU

Eternally dedicated to Carl F. Cook

When night has come
as the cricket sings,
I will remember.

Tomorrow as the warmth of the sun
melts away morning's frigid dew,
I will remember.

As your children grow
when I see you in them,
I will remember.

Each time I close my eyes
dreaming of what could have been,
I will remember.

When my Soul aches for the one I called
brother and friend,
until my time on this earth comes to
an end,
I will remember you.

THE DAY THE OCEAN RAN DRY

ETERNALLY DEDICATED TO WAYNE ALLEN BAILEY

A small town girl
In a great big world
Discovering where she'd find
Life's song
Each day she now wakes, traveling on
Even though he's gone.

Courage innately knew him
He passed it on to her
Born in her own strength
Finding serenity in a mirrored flame,
Love is a motion
Not just a name.

Oceans continue to reach the shores
As blue-hued skies stand still
Memories continue echoing from our
haven
With each remembrance I am filled.

Our hands still embracing
As your Spirit was released,
Some Loves dissolve
Others never cease.

E TERNAL

If the sky above
can be endless and blue,
the oceans depths too...

Then I can be.

E YE OF LIGHT

Upon its radiant beams

That cast down to the deep sea

Loves rays of fortitude

Carry all through solitude

Waiver not into the lonely night

For God holds all that is the Light

Cloaks within wraps of lustrous gold

For mercy warms the deepest cold

Rise up this morning without haste

Days are fortune, do not waste

The sun shinning bright

Bare skin to its rays embrace

Receive all that can transcend,

Welcome beauty in.

The Rose (Tupac)

For Tupac Amaru Shakur

June 16, 1971 – September 13, 1996

Beautiful bright-eyed man
Your Light eternally shines
Even as a child, you held a kingly mind
Effortless wisdom from your words
did ring

Young old Soul —infinite
Even then you knew truths
Delivering them to us on time
With poetic rhythm and rhyme

They took you from us far too soon,
As they have taken so many before.

Though they've tried,
Your purpose they cannot obscure
With each day its power grows
Roots fortified, deep, secure

Not merely cracking open the window of
knowledge
You boldly busted wide the door
Exposing for all to see the shame
Of the hidden players in the game

Your message —it is getting louder
As Prophets always do
More than twenty years later
The essence of you possesses strength to
attune

Your verses invincibly stream
From countless speakers and rooms
Destiny turning up the volume
Blaring your unmistakable booms.

Rolled down summer windows
As folks cruise the street
Echoing your apperceptions of rhyme
They haven't skipped a beat…

The Rose That Grew From Concrete.

To Sail

Bought a new guitar
Forgot I never learned to play
Wrote another Love song
Where my words went astray

Whispers in the wind
Tell me it's time to fly
Yet when I pack my bag
My Soul begins to cry

Mirroring the moments
Of Love's eternal flame
An ocean of memories
Like a tidal wave untamed

Who am I to complain…

I have a book of poems
To ease my circus mind
Retracing the steps
Of life's melodic rhyme

What I seek to find
Has always been within me
Intertwined
Within my unconscious mind

Time weaves a thousand tales
Of which I do not wish to tell
Instead I'll focus on the memories
Until I'm compelled to sail.

BE A LIGHT

When you don't know what else to do,
be a Light.

~

PART II

MIDNIGHT BLUES

MELANCHOLY WINE

I was looking for you

Under the star glazed night

Wandering through hallows

Abandoned vineyards of devotion

Filled with visions of deserted memories

Once full of grace

Replaced with the echoes of silence

As I retraced pathways voyaged

Legs weary with time

Reminiscing and melancholy intertwined

Quenching the thirst with a lilac wine.

E TERNALLY UNTITLED NO. 1

What do you do when words have lost
their meaning
When they fall upon ears that no
longer hear
Frustration consumes as you reach to find
Meaning in the meaningless, security in a
fear driven world
In an age where lies are said to set
you free
Believing that a positive mention will
release the chains' decree
In stillness, thoughts do not have power to
bombard
In isolation, the sharpness of words do not
leave one in shards.

HUMANITY

I Loved so hard
I fell upon the ground
Splitting open with agony
I bled out into the world

Emptying myself in wailing
Unto absolute exhaustion
Why can't you see the Love
It is all around

Blinded by mirrors
Seeing only the self
Fears have trapped you
As you sing of your false freedom

We harm one another so
Without thought of the dead
Floating around us
Our weapons as vast as the sea

We do what feels good
With no thought of
Generations to come
As our ancestors once did

Today it is me —only me
Everyone has a pulpit
Even those who use theirs
For twisted truths of their own

Distraction, destruction, device
Vomiting words
Into the darkness
Of a digital abyss

What we are leaving our children
A disaster torn village
Burnt bridges
Singed souls

The world is over
God is dead, Nietzsche said
We have killed Him
Murderers of all murderers

That which creates
Cannot be silenced
Our salvation awaits within,
We have lost our way, the way

Quickly run back to yourself
Before it is too late
Before there is no more
Bloom to water

Shut the doors
Quiet the world around you
There is a message
A purpose crying in your spirit

Breathe life into it
Nurture it with Love
Swim in its emerald waters
Let it saturate every pore

Listen so carefully
You mustn't whisper a word,
Make the world a better place
Begin within your innerspace.

U NLIVED LIFE

In shadows she walks
Avoiding the light
Within it live memories
She did not write
Longing in silence
In this life left undone
Reaching for penance
Avoiding the sun.

THE WOUND

The one that is so deep it burns
its fire never quenched
no matter how many
slow liquid flames that flow
down a throat choking in anguish,
it persists

tearing slowly at you like the
tiny hairs bound to a bandage
that torture as they are pulled
inch by inch.

Will the day come when
the softness of new skin
allow it to mend,
for even the wind causes
the wound to heat.

A NONYMITY

Putting my heart to bed

Safer in slumber than dead

Warred through years

Birthed in shame

You called it love, I call it pain

Compassion pulled me toward you

Believing in you impelled my hell

Illusions of holding you up

When we had already failed.

THE VINES

Time and distance continue to reveal
While words escape the emotion
Vines of disbelief entangle
Strangle the mind
Suffocate the Soul, left unconsoled

Remembering words spoken in spirit
Condition rare, trust sincere
Belief in another
Holy walks through our minds
Turning to find the choking by those vines

Ejection of promises incite reflections of
doubt
Illusions once held of sustenance
Asphyxiate throughout
Living in a world where
It's all too easy to walk out.

~

PART III

ENTERS: BROKEN MAN

D IG WHAT I SAY

I will Love you deeply
I will Love you raw
Don't get my devotion twisted
Conspiring for my fall

Bare ass to the sun
Your sins I will shine
If you forget I am Love
While trampling over mine

Now dig what I say
As in, see what I hear
You have no conscience
It succumbed to fear

People aren't envious
They see straight through
The endless masquerade
Fraudulent posturing you do

True confidence
Effortlessly glimmers
Hidden from heedless fools…

In pumping your ego
Your crown loses its jewels.

HIS BARREN SOUL

You say it was by accident
Yet you purposely broke in
You said, *isn't it lovely*
Then why does it feel like sin

Transforming bread from stone
I fed you safety to atone
Offering a haven, seeing you were alone
Where others failed you, I was home

Your lies, don't they haunt
As your backbiting taunts
Are you not tired of the hunt
Of the erroneous stardom flaunt

My name the song you repeatedly
compose
With fantasies you fraudulently disclose
Singing my name time after time
Is your obsession exposed

The crime of your words
Twisting records of truth
Burning ballads to ash
As you continually bash,
...it's inevitable you crash.

Until redemption comes
On stormy days, stay inside
For your unrooted Soul
Is destined for landslide.

Dusty from the Years

Tortured by his fears
This man has lived a thousand years
With a damaged mind he rambles
Leaving those he encounters in shambles
Ominous shadows weigh heavy

Addicted to misery
Inflicted by the brief taste of fame
He can't find his way to free
Too busy putting others down
Never able to attain his own crown

Spinning deceptions from silk
Stolen by lovely women
Lured into his web
He sneaks in with charm
Gaslighted they're misled

Reckless he inflicts his victims
Exploiting their genuine desire
To protect and save,
Manipulation is his name
Injecting venom his parlor game

He's dusty from the years
They've dried up all his tears
Now he's bitter and cold
A Soul long ago sold
Terrified to grow old.

DEVIL DANCE

When devils reappear in your life, do not dance with them. Write them away in the words of your poetry. Breathe them out in the notes of your song.

Do not entertain pain.

～

PART IV

ATHENA RISING

Exodus

Write his venom out of your bones, wash
treachery from your skin. Forgive your
misjudgment, you simply let the wrong
one in. Purify your heart expelling all sins.
This is the place to begin... the exodus.

R EVIVAL

Consumed by the blandness

Of your caustic ways

Overwrought in the travail

Of a thousand weary days

As you savor the fault

For the dulling of my gold

An ember kept warm

My melancholy Soul

A universe poignant

Rousing me to wake

Fortified by passion

Revival my fate.

Not My Home

This is not my home
Been riding the waves
Awaiting the day
Until ready to move on
Collecting memories to forget
Savoring the days of Love
Before regret

I can forgive, forgetting eludes
Not willing to live
In the shadows of disaccord
I will flow with this river
Until it lands me upon the shore
No longer waiting on another
For permission to soar

Releasing all that entombed
That had taken over me
Returning to the woman inside
Before self-sacrifice consumed
Delivering my survival
Surrendering to the nature of rebirth
I am returning to the womb.

R ETURN TO YOU

You used to be so strong
Baby what went wrong

They told you to take a left
You knew it wasn't right

When did you lose it mama
When did you give up the fight

Remnants of that girl
Ready to take on the world

A toss turned to a twirl
Eye am still rooting for that girl

She's there, look harder
Break the shell —break the shell

It's created your jail,
Eye paid your bail

Driving up in a white limousine
Purple and white flowers

They're all for you
Now believe in yourself

What you can do, if it weren't true
Would eye be here for you

This ain't no game.

FOUND

Beloved, you are not lost.
Rub your eyes, turn around,
to your wonder you are found.

You have been here
all along blinded by the lie
you were not enough.

Breathe in, embrace
your impeccable beauty.
The One you have searched for
you now see.

You have the secret,
you are set free.
Be brilliant.

G OLDEN GIRL

Golden girl of wonder
heart bright,
remove the shade
keeping you from
your own Light.

F LY WITH ME

Inspired by Clarissa Pinkola Estés, PhD

Dedicated to Stevie Nicks

Does it grip you
Does it shift you
Does it make you feel all right
Does it fly with you through
The darkness of your solitary night

Does it purge you
Urge you
Crave you
Aim you
Ever toward the Light

Can it traverse you the distance
Even without sight
Can it fade the pain
As it leads you through wayward fields
As the wise old owl at midnight

Feel me, see me
Fly with me in the night
Beneath the moon's amber glow
Converging
Inside of me
Gravity lets go
As we surrender to this flow
Will you overcome your fright
Fly with me into the night

A once clear trail scatters
None of it really matters

As you're picked up
By all knowing winds
Knowing with faith
You'll land exactly
Where you're meant to begin

Wings wrap around you closely
Like a second skin
Take it in
It's no sin
If it brings you closer to Him
Love lifting you higher
As you begin
As you begin
As you begin once again

Feel me, see me
Fly with me in the night
Beneath the moon's amber glow
Converging inside of me
Gravity lets go
As we surrender to this flow
Will you overcome your fright
Fly with me into the night

Now hold it
Your heart
Enclose it within your hands
Caress it
Reassess it
As you realign with your zen

The fertile remnants left
From life's ebbs and flows
Nurturing

Guiding
Just where your Soul's to go

Tell me your secrets
The ones only you know
Take me to your trove
Where your true treasures grow

Feel me, see me
Fly with me in the night
Beneath the moon's amber glow
Converging inside of me
Gravity lets go
As we surrender to this flow

Will you overcome your fright
Fly with me into the night
Fly with me into the night
Fly with me into the night.

INNER STRENGTH

Life's had its battles
I've stood strong
Living with no regrets
Always rising to carry on

No failures, only lessons
This journey has made me who I am
Experience my teacher
Grace my closest friend

In the darkest of hours
Knowing I will have wings to fly
Love guiding my direction
While change stands closely by

All that once seemed wrong
Now shines brightly from within
Reflecting a Soul's growth
Inner strength to transcend.

L ULLABIED WHOLE

Tame this gentle heart
Overcome with fear
Sever the embryonic
Longing to be near
Return to me rejuvenated
Preparing for the new
Following the journey
What else is there to do
To walk around the desert
For a thousand years
To return to the ocean
Salt tinged tears
Singing a song of healing
Lullabied whole
Igniting passions
Of a heart turned cold
Bitterness numbs the palate
Forgiveness flavors the Soul
Enlightenment carries the spirit
Love pays the toll
Sing a song of healing
Strum chords of refrain
Releasing notes while dreaming
Never to return this way again.

THE CLEANSING

Cleanse yourself of what no longer serves you. And I'm not talking about running from doing your work. No dear One, there is too much of that mentality in today's society; escapism through blaming others, playing the victim. Face your demons. Do your work. Then, empowered, move on when you know you've done all you can and evolving has been refused.

Love's The Way

Often people come in
Not knowing the rules
Can make a wise one
Into an accidental fool
The romantic love trip
Turned cliché

Darling, true Love seeks
To bestow serenity
Upon the darkest of days
If a lover doesn't know this
Why would you ask them to stay

Your heart is no place for child's play
There's another way
Never allow mere emotion
To lead you astray.

The Shift

No longer needing approval, appreciation
or validation's relief,
only the Soul's —my Soul.
The experience received in the depths of
my existence the only motivation required.
Tranquil moments of creativity carved
intricately in intimate places, smoothed
like rock worn by the rushing stream.
That is when I knew I had changed
—when it was more for me than it was
for you.

B ut Then, I Rise

The best of us fall
Courage is found
In returning home
Tossed about
In seas of rage

Knowing one motion
May resurrect the sage
Releasing its power within
A single reflective sigh
Take the pain, burying it alive

Be gentle with you
Be gentle with me
Do not force to swim
Against a tumultuous sea
It devours spirit and bone whole

Surrender is not self betrayal
It redirects your sails.
I fall, but then I rise.

S TRONG SHE STOOD

INSPIRED BY & FOR PRIANA APLIN

DEDICATED TO RACHELLE FEARS-NEAL & TONIA CRAGUN

Strong she stood
Believing she did not sway
Nor did she sit still in waiting
Merely anticipating the day
Courage knew her
Grace often would stop by
Enabling her wing to heal
Knowing soon she'd need to fly
No matter the situation
Or the demons that stood at bay
She rested in His arms
Believing He would pave her way
An angel, a sister
A beautiful friend
Dedication to her truest Love,
Faith that has no end.

To My Sisters

1.

You are the precious child of something
greater than the human mind holds ability
to comprehend. You are the Mother of all.
You are the child of an ancestral line far
too many have lost connection with.

Shades of brown, yellow, red, olive, peach
or pale —we are Sisters, you are my
Sister. Until we realize our Sisterhood to
all it is impossible to truly know ourselves
singularly.

Women have a history in a social structure
as unequal yet we hear the call deep within
our being, knowing the power we hold
within our touch, within our minds eyes
—within our Love.

We hold the ability to stir emotions so
deep and powerful they cause the pulse to
quicken or calm.

Women have been uniquely designed by
the Source of Creation to give birth to
beating hearts that give home to the Soul.

We are the Mothers of our planet. We are
conduits of healing and through the

receiving of that healing we have the potential to teach and pass it on to the next.

We understand what healing truly is: not a quick fix, but an experience of wholeness.

2.

When we accept the bodies we live in as the magnificent Temples they are, however scarred from battle or wounded from grief and pains they may be, we open up within a portal of Light that beams more brightly than the brightest star, when we understand who and what we are.

It pains me to see my fellow Sister beat herself down because of a number on her dress size, an insecurity of not realizing her true beauty or misunderstanding of her vast worth.

Even the most beautifully adorned too often see imperfections instead of the Goddess. The word "goddess" means "a woman who is adored." Yet we are all too often hyper-vigilant of what we feel we lack.

To not be in the realm of self-Love is a space of unknowing. It is an energetic pocket seething with lies. It is in this place we are out of alignment with the truth and make choices that lead us out of our integrity.

Let our goal be to leave reminders of who we are so we may not stay long when we enter into those moments of unknowing.

Let us be vulnerable enough to go to a trusted Sister and ask for a reminder. Let us Love one another with grace and strength.

3.

Loving ourselves authentically is perhaps the greatest of challenges. I ask you to look at yourself through the same eyes of Love you have for those you hold most dear. We are often the most critical with ourselves.

Today, take the time to embrace what those who truly Love and appreciate you experience when they look into your eyes. Take great care of your Temple by nourishing it —today, not once you lose that extra five pounds —today. Love it today.

Today, Sister, I ask you to sit in silence. Let all thoughts and the minutia of daily living go —remember who you are. Give way for the inner voice to whisper its own Love letter to your Soul.

Remember the little girl who still resides within, let her come out and play. When we do, it's amazing what she can remind and re-teach us.

Be mindful, in the moment, with awareness that this body is temporal, but the spirit eternal.

Mother yourself. Nurture your spirit. Breathe in gentleness and allow it to saturate your being.

Know that each choice you make and life you touch literally changes eternity.

Begin with your own.

4.

Embrace your sensual spirit. Do not abuse your own body or allow another to for the body and spirit as we know are undeniably intertwined.

The enlightenment that can come from the sharing and embracing of our sensuality in spirit is beyond words. May we all take the care to entrust our Souls and Temples only with those who also know and practice this as truth.

The world exploits a woman's sexuality, but we have the power to direct our own personal energies and claim our power. Standing in this power, we give rise to truth and lower level energies may not reside near us —or in us.

In this we instantly and effortlessly stand apart from the norm. We set standards for all those we come into contact. We give the gift to our young Sister to know she is a jewel to be adored, not a trinket to be tossed amongst others trivially.

In this we offer gratitude to the ancestral line of Mothers who have come before giving us life. Feel your feet firmly planted on the earth and imagine the deep roots of the tree of life.

Envision these deep roots intertwining far below, embedded in rich nurturing soil that provides enduring strength... and when needed, remember to find shelter within its shade and restorative branches. Be still.

Remember. We know so much, often it is a matter of remembering versus learning.

Look above you into the sky and recognize the expansive majesty and mysteries of how great an opportunity to be on Mother Earth in this, our universe. Recognize the universe and your part in it. It is beyond miraculous.

Above all, know my dear Sister you are
Loved and in that you are Love.

Commit to a path of its mastery.

~

PART V

INTERLUDE: WEEPING RAINBOW

4 U

Dreaming in the Heavens
Plucking stars like ripe berries
To sweetly feed to U
Tenderly preparing a princely feast
To see U through
Any journey long or brief
I give to U today, my undying Love

I wish U could have stayed.

-April 26, 2016

Coup My Flowers

Ownership and power once held complete,
my creations flowing, the world was
sweet.
Then the day came…
Old friends, now I am for sale.

I gave you a career, abundance flowed.
My creations, not your own,
still I gave you a seat near my throne.
Until for you it was the end of the road,
then you kicked and screamed
told secrets and lies…
some truths as seen through your eyes.

Now the spotlight has returned.
Are your egos glad?
Let me get my piece of all that he had.
Want my fifteen too, after all, I'm due.
He's finally left this empty room.

In my name and your hunger,
making money off my death
calling it "tribute,"
yet, you know when you came calling
I gave that idea the boot.

In my departure you decide in a beat,
Let's go on the road.
The mourners need a feast; they'll eat.
What will be delivered,
regurgitated foul rotted fruit from my vine;

in your mind, it's your time.

Those ones in my circle
who now sell their tales,
sharing my stories with vivid detail.
I see all you're doing.
This bittersweet taste of fame,
carrying out your agendas
in my royal name.

This revolution is about something more,
had to get your foot in the door.
It was shut for so long,
wasn't it thirty years?
I hope you shed at least
a few purple tears.

A stage was set on April 21st
where some would parade with thirst.
True colors flying around and about,
most have already struck out.

God's stage set to show who you truly are,
all while knowing,
it was I who made you a star.

PRINCE

I have no desire to sing of purple rain
Only want to see your smile again
Laughter to replace the tears
Feel your presence near
Blessed are those who knew
What a playful glance infused

In your transit composing
A universal arpeggio
Reverberating throughout Heaven
Serenading eternal vibrato
Only heightening the longing
To be near your flow

The windows are open
Welcoming the breath of your name
A cascading chorus of fragrant petals
Knowing life will never be the same
Transitioning far too soon
Leaving this universe out of tune

I rest in between the lines of lyric
Where your memory thrives
Living forever without effort
Throughout all space and time
Your absence left the vinyl skipping
Interrupting a Divine rhyme

For those whom you've touched
Your telepathic eloquence,
Your cherished ethereal ways
We speak with our silence
As we continue to count the days.

Weeping Willow

The weeping willow cries no more
Where there was once only a wall
She has opened a door
There is no lock
…she has been here before

Eye wide open
Seeing into forevermore
No longer keeping score
Frees the Soul to be adored

I use to live for others
Setting them free
Never did I see the glass
Reflecting back at me

Somehow you effortlessly
Gave me the key to
Wiping dry the tears
Of my weeping tree.

Is My Love For You

Firmly rooted
As that aged weeping willow
Seated majestically atop the hill
Deep as sapphire seas
Immense as the Milky Way
As far as the eye can see
Fragrant as the freshly
Open bud of the rose
Sweet as the song
The whippoorwill echoes
Soft as an angels touch
Strong as ancient mountains
Precious as the rarest of jewels
As long as time can be,
Eons past eternity
Is my Love for you.

Violets For You

I felt you in the caress
Of the butterflies wing
The promise you would never end
Whispered by a gentle breeze
Under skies of eternal spring
Wildflowers draped in dew
Spirit sang its song today,
She sang it just For You.

Night beckons memories
Mourning's gentle pain
I hear you say
From pain what is there to gain
Bring then in its place
Tangerine's creative spark
Wakeful mornings overjoyed
Soothing broken hearts

Singing your sweet melody
Born a royal frame of design
Harmony consistent
Without need of time
Every day I will sing of you
In a violet frame of mind.

FLOWERS IN MY GARDEN

The flowers in my garden
Each and every one
Soaking in the warmth
From the risen Son
When I miss your colors
When I'm feeling blue
Sitting with my flowers
Brings me back to you
Seasons take them
Yet they return every time
True to the essence
Of nature's rhyme
Walking through my garden
Life continues to grow
Bursting into melodic hues
Each velvet petal a reluctant adieu
As I welcome another dawn
They say what is lost is never gone
So my cherished one, I carry on
As I reminisce of you.

~

PART VI

SONG OF VENUS

M OTH TO A FLAME

Drawn to you like a moth to the flame
At first I was concerned my wings
Would be singed
Now I am fearless —consume me

Bring me into you.

Secret Sanctuary

I know I can trust you,
I wish I had known then
Your aura so true
I didn't know
Where to begin
You threw me for a loop
Weren't all up in my shoop

You were a beautiful green
Peaceful, serene
Had I known then what I do now
We'd both be better
No questioning how
I could have healed your heart
And sealed my own

We would have created
A sanctuary, a home

Spiritual friend,
You stayed until past the end

Baby, I'm still around
Remember your heart is Holy ground

Love harmonizing through sound
That's where I can be found.

PERFECT TUNE

You can play the key of me
Sounds like a heavenly symphony
Notes of sweet embrace
Combining to play this
Sweet enchanting chord
This is what Love is

Rhythm's so sweet
Savoring every note
I can listen to the sweet, sweet
Sounds of your melody
Until sound is no more
Have you ever felt more adored

H IS LOVE

I was always right there
Reading your words
Tasting your thoughts
With me you were never lost
I knew the places you went to
Where you were going and sent to
It's not always what you think
Had I taken a sip
I couldn't have stopped at a single drink
We did it right, dry your tears
One day we'll be back together
For a thousand years.

Bring to Me

Bring to me
All you want to be
Allow yourself
Set it free
For your safety lies
Within my wings

You can take the next step
For if you fall
I will be there
Before you call
To mend any wound
Banish any care

If not for you
Where would I go
When life is untrue
When it's heartless and cruel
My bright shining star
That's what you are.

TRANSCENDENTLY

Spiraling light slowed dims
Encapsulating our night
Beloved release all that
Refuses to allow you to swim
In this expansive cosmic sea
Together is when
We are truly set free
I pen poetic peaces with you
When you move with me
Silver slivers of moon
Shower us with crystal tunes
Strumming transiently
As we make a wish
Upon a shooting star
We will always be this free
Beloved keep creating with me
Our Love knows, it grows
Within this sweet chorus
In each breath our lyric flows…
Transcendentally.

Ultimate Mixtape

For tonight, hold me
Let tomorrow take care of itself
Erase the messages
Left on my mind
Let us record the Love
We've refined
Sound so divine
Got me hitting rewind
Repeating lyrical lines
Got our rhyme moving
In double-time it's so sublime

I have to let you know,
you are my favorite lover.

MIDNIGHT WAVES

As the waves collide
Can you hear their sighs
The moon their master
Not knowing what it is they're after
Chasing the shore, forevermore
Moonbeams illuminate the night
As we lay beneath
A sea of its crystal lights
We count past a thousand
Energy pulsating through
The vessel of you
The darkness runs
Sheltered by countless suns
Transcended to another place
Ecstasy frozen in time
Where faces fade, our spirits soar
All while our bodies never leave the shore.

Amber Rain

Close your eyes as I caress your brow
Whispering euphoric words
Never to be spoken again
Belonging only to you
My lover, my friend

As the sun unhurriedly departs
Raindrops peacefully fall
Revealing secrets kept from my heart,
I'll tell you where I'm going
If you'll tell me how to start

Your words too fall softly
As that sunset champagne
They speak of my pain
Cleansing as an early April rain
Ridding abiding refrain

Under the amber rain…

In Slumber

Carpets of velvet green
Skies of burnt umber
Upon a bed of dandelions
I meet my dreams in slumber

A waning moon
Comforts this heart of mine
As a stream of crystal tinged waters
Reflect words left to find

Songbirds harmonize
Their song to sing
As I dream of moments yet to be

Rose petals fall from above
I reminisce how your body fit mine
Like an inviting satin glove

Smooth to the touch
Warm to the mind
Embracing bodies
Souls intertwined

Carpets of velvet green
Skies of burnt umber
Upon a bed of dandelions
I meet my dreams in slumber.

I Breathe You In

Sensual laced kisses
Touches of adoration
The smell of musk
I breathe you in
Lips of velvet
Eyes of earth
Strength of wisdom
I breathe you in
Hands of creativity
Mind of serenity
Spirit of truth
I breathe you in

My Love,
My friend
There is no beginning
There need be no end.

PASSION PEN

Overflowing with the ache of an
intoxicating potency from impassioned
words not yet birthed…

COME TO ME

Close your eyes
Listen only to the breath
Between the sighs
Without touching
Without one word being said
Truth drenches us in this bed

Full embrace
Souls intertwine
Not knowing where
Your flesh ends
Then turns into mine
Bodies can't keep us apart
Your Love lives in me

Eternal and pure
Created to endure
Into this world
We were born
Fragile and torn
Sent to one another
We are two in the same
Wearing one name

Remembering wounds mend,
and true Love never ends.

Once

Once you've allowed yourself
To look deep into my eyes
Once you've been between these thighs
Passion for all others dies
Once your Love sends my Soul to cry
Once upon your neck I've placed my sigh
Once,
Once in awhile
Every century or two
There comes a Love
This true

Once you've had all
That money buys
Once you've found everlasting emptiness
In a stranger's eyes
Once you know the loneliness
Of a rainy day
Of Love given
Then taken away
Once you have done these
For the final time
Once you translate reason to rhyme
That is when the truth of what I offer
Will shine

Once in your mind's Eye
You see me
And all that could be
I am all you are ever going to need.

Your Rain

Let the winds blow
Let the waters rage
For now I am in your arms
In only you am I engaged

The smell of your wild ocean
Intoxicating assuage
I willfully drown
In the rousing of your rain.

MAN IN TIME

He was beautiful
In a raw sort of way
Skin of chestnut
A smile that lit a thousand rooms
His stride had its own swagger

He was not to be denied
One glance raised to surface
Fire, burning —a throb
Hand reaching out with purpose
Fingers dark, long and strong

Presence so effortlessly seductive
Diffusing from every pore
A fragrance I had never known
He wasn't a player
Just a lover of many

There were no games or promises
Only a moment in time
When I had no doubt
I was his —and he was mine
We ravished one another

Until the sun rose
Cadence sumptuous as prose
We talked about life until all
Questions were left unposed
He went his way and I mine

I've never been the same
Since that man in time.

H IS EYES

His eyes called me nearer
As senses begged stay away
His hand massaging my longing
I pulled, swayed, then stayed

Vibrations coursing through flesh
Like thunder on a rainy day
His presence allows no drowning
As we lay

Illusions of separateness fading
Drenched in midnights dew
Lips dripping with lyric softly say,

Just as the leaves know
they belong to the trees,
so do I to you.

M AJESTIC MOUNTAINS

Majestic mountains hover above us
Under a navy sky
Below them both
We lay in tall grasses
This Love making us high

A crystal stream flows
My river does the same
Ensconced in your aura
Entranced by your frame
Passion so erotic, impossible to tame

Legs wrapped around you
I feel my back rise
Fully taking you in
I moan animalistic cries
Bringing me to rapture

It feels Heaven is nigh
I savor your nectar,
Lips between my thighs
Tongue making love to me
Submerging me in ecstasy

I pray this night never ends
As I dream under an early moon,
A single tear forms
Then escapes from my eye
For I know I will wake soon.

S PIRITUAL DESTINY

As you rise
Body heavy on mine
I breathe in your essence
Rhythmic melodic, vibe divine
Entranced by your fragrance
Frankincense and myrrh combined
Reminiscent of ancient gods
Transcending me to a place
Where angels trod
Heightening my spirit
By the mere touch of your hand
Understanding this night
I am your woman, you are my man

Seeing deep into my eyes
Beyond what others can
Since you entered,
Life has been changed
Free, tranquilly sane
Unchained to life's games
We —two in the same
Taken to a higher plane

Pleasure so intense it shakes the Soul
Faith in one another, radiantly bold
It has been foretold
In another place and time
There is a reason, there is a rhyme
Do you find it sublime
These two Souls did find such like minds

Given a perfect place to intertwine
At just the right time

Amazed at the view
Eternal, fateful
A prophecy come true.

My Man

DEDICATED TO THE LOVE OF MY LIFE

He's the one who holds my hand, when the ground beneath me trembles.

He incites balance with merely the touch of his hand upon the small of my back.

He has opened my eyes to things that dwell within me; some I did not like, so I do my work to clear them.

Others made me fall deeply in Love with myself — and him.

He calls my name in both my dreams and nightmares to remind me there is no storm I cannot navigate.

He reminds me of where I came from while not deterring where I am going.

A reflection of what nature's beauty holds, he finds his peace in simplicity.

He reminds me that all too often I give too much of myself to others while not saving a portion for myself.

When needed he fiercely reminds me of this; again, again and again.

When I overanalyze a situation his eyes look deeply into my own, allowing me to once again find my center.

He fires me up and cools me down all in timely ways that strengthen.

He injects my world with the sweetness of laughter.

Through every phase of life we have inevitably found our way —even in ravaging storms as encircling vultures calculated their attacks.

Often the most exhaustive times of our journey unearthed elevated abilities to endure and soar.

Ups and downs and emotional merry go rounds; we are on this ride together.

Velvet Tongue

Hours turn to seconds
As I melt into you
Skin merges
Fluidity converges
Felt in a way
This mind can't comprehend
Only knowing the Soul longs for it
Again, and again

Addiction of a drink
That burns as a summer sun
Now do it once more,
Touch me with your velvet tongue

Arched back in felicity
Kissing me
With eyes full of passion
Watching over me
As you send me to ecstasy…

Bodies

Don't lay next to me, lay on me
So close my skin can drink you in.

Gold

Rummaging through the years
Searching for the moment
Knowing in my Soul
The universe held you
Being in this world
All too often lonely and cold
I held on to the hope
One day I would find my gold
Running through my days
One by one
To arrive at the now
You see, my Soul always knew
Its gold was in you
Precious is the day
Your path crossed my way
Exquisite is this Love
Out sparkling a king's ransom in jewels
This Love, a Love without rules
Built only on the foundation
Of all that is pure
Requiring only our presence
For this Love to endure
Piece by piece
Hearts become whole
Since the day I found
The other half of my Soul.

S UNSHINE

My Sunshine walks in the room
Smothering all gloom
I've watched the sun rise
Just by gazing into his eyes
In his arms lives calm
His words poetic
Poignant as psalms
Mesmerizing my Soul
His nurturing makes me whole
A King among mere men
Wisdom that transcends
Stirring the fire
Fueling endless desires
Lifting life higher
When he is near
Earthly fears disappear
For there lives the truest Love
With him I can be completely free
As the God of the universe
Intended it to be
The decree was written
Prophecy fulfilled
Delivering spiritual ecstasy
Deep as the roots
Of the knowledge tree
Bright as the sun
We've only just begun.

Let Me Break It Down

Let me break it down
While no one's around
Just the moon above
Shouting down
Only fools fall in Love
But you, you Baby
Fit me like that worn
Warm leather glove
Know every curve
Embracing so tight
Making our hearts heavy
With Light
No end in sight
Knowing somehow
It's going to work out right
Being all I can be
You cause me to see
Baby I was made for you,
You were made for me

Let me break it down
While no one's around
This Love we've found.

L AST DANCE

One last dance
Through this romance
The moment has come
The party is done

We beg the DJ
For one more song
In hopes our Love
Will linger on

The lights are low
We're dancing slow
Love, we must go
It was fun, now it's done

Like sand we fall through
One another's hands
Knowing our hearts
Will never be the same
I softly whisper your name
As two hearts exclaim
For all eternity our sweet Love remains.

So It Shall Be

Late at night
When the day is done
After there is no trace remaining
Of the orange evening sun
I go to a place deep in my Soul
In that place
You are there
Awaiting me
To quench every care

Slowly I kiss
Every inch of you
Doing only for you
Those things I thought
I would never do
With joy I do them
Again and again
Feeling only purity
In this Love without sin

As your sighs of passion
Caress my neck
In ecstasy
You in me
I am no longer one
I am so much more
Experiencing Love
My body and Soul
Have never known before

The world outside
Need not exist
For all that is needed
To survive is your kiss
Follow me Baby
To the place
Meant for only you and I
That place in our spirits
That shall never die

No need to be afraid
Hold on tightly to me
The universe wrote it,
So it shall be.

R ARE

Rare is a woman like me
The Love I offer
Sets captives free
Sends men to their knees,
In ecstasy
Accept this Love
You will feel like royalty
God, you, and I make three
This is how it is meant to be
The way I Love is how
God Himself intended
Love to be
Supreme greatness
Waiting only for you
There is no other
Who makes me yearn as you do
You will experience majesty
Once you are inside of me

It is meant to be,
Set this jewel free.

~

PART VII

SACRED IS THE PRAYER

CHILD OF GOD

I pray you be cloaked in grace
May the Angels embrace
Each day as you wake
May their hand you take

Turn from a world
Drenched in confusion
Until clarity returns
Removing all illusion

Child of God,
You are Loved
Beyond comprehension
Set upon mountains
Otherworldly dimensions

Reach for nothing
As the stars are your pillows
Know all required
Rests within Heavenly billows
Moonbeams shower your mind
Reminding you it's all easy to find
When you let go, you align

Child of God,
Rest easy today
For nothing can be taken
When you're willing to give it away

Open your heart
In wisdom and might
So it is written:
Wise as a serpent, tender as a dove.

Child of God,
Do and receive all things with Love.

Acknowledgments

Thank you's do not suffice in expressing my heartfelt gratefulness to my entire Tribe. You lift me up and surround me with Love. Your names alone could fill a masterpiece of poetry.

Special thanks to:

C.C. Allentini for a soft space to land. It's not just anyone who understands the paths we have both traveled.

Dr. Margena A. Christian, for your encouragement to see this through and the years of getting me through the mourning. I will never forget.

Michael Van Huffel, if not for you the days would seem too long to bear. Even through your own storms you beam light into my world.

Meredith Young-Sowers, my mentor and Spiritual Mother, how grateful I am to be blessed by the gracious Love of your deep heart.

Tonia Cragun, for being the best friend a girl could have. We all need someone who has been there since day one.

Doug Powers, while thankful for your editorial skills it is your tremendously skilled heart that sets you apart.

To the exceptional artistic designer Jesse Hayes, I offer my sincerest gratitude for cover design only you could create so effortlessly and perfectly for this book. Your patience and authenticity bless my life.

To my parents I give thanks for your Love and support. Giving birth to a poetic heart can be a difficult labour.

To Anthony, for your Love, loyalty and devotion; while there are sonnets eternal, our Love exceeds the capability of mere word.

To Steven Pressfield, one of my author heroes, for sending me his book *The Artist's Journey* in the most divine timing; I am forever thankful.

In remembrance of Mother Maya Angelou, whom I did not have the honor of meeting in the physical, I wholeheartedly express my sincerest offerings of gratefulness for the compass her words have, and continue to be, throughout my life.

And to you dear reader, my Beloveds who dare to Love in and beyond brokenness; the most courageous act of the warrior's heart, the strength to transform pain to beauty —the alchemists you are.

GIN LOVE THOMPSON, PhD is an award-winning poet, writer, spoken word artist, activist, ancient wisdom teacher, psychotherapist and nationally recognized relationship specialist. Gin has written courses for major holistic mind, body, and spirit resources such as DailyOM.com. Her expert relationship advice has been featured on the TODAY Show, Huffington Post, Everyday Health, Chicago Tribune, Prevention, Glamour, Women's Health, Fitness, Travel + Leisure, Men's Health, Woman's Day and more.

She is an eminent authority on creativity and the expressive arts transformational effects having presented on their therapeutic practice internationally. Creative expression through verse has been an innate part of Gin's life since childhood. This book of poetry is a rebirth. After achieving noteworthy success in her professional fields her focus is rededicated to her roots of poetry and writing.

For more information, visit:
www.ginlovethompson.com

CPSIA information can be obtained
at www.ICGtesting.com
Printed in the USA
LVHW012359160120
643834LV00003B/44